A TRUE BOOK™

India

SUNITA APTE

Children's Press®
An Imprint of Scholastic Inc.
New York Toronto London Auckland Sydney
Mexico City New Delhi Hong Kong
Danbury, Connecticut

Content Consultant

Sophie Hawkins, Ph.D.
Adjunct Professor of Religion
Hofstra University
Hempstead, NY

Library of Congress Cataloging-in-Publication Data

Apte, Sunita.
  India / by Sunita Apte.
     p. cm. — (A true book)
  Includes index.
  ISBN-13: 978-0-531-16890-5 (lib. bdg.)   978-0-531-21357-5 (pbk.)
  ISBN-10: 0-531-16890-5 (lib. bdg.)   0-531-21357-9 (pbk.)
  1. India—Juvenile literature. I. Title. II. Series.

  DS407.A744 2009
  954—dc22   2008014786

Produced by Weldon Owen Education Inc.

1 2 3 4 5 6 7 8 9 10 R 18 17 16 15 14 13 12 11 10 09

Find the Truth!

Everything you are about to read is true *except* for one of the sentences on this page.

Which one is **TRUE**?

T or F   Many Indians don't eat meat.

T or F   The elephant is India's national animal.

Find the answers in this book.

Contents

THE **BIG** TRUTH!

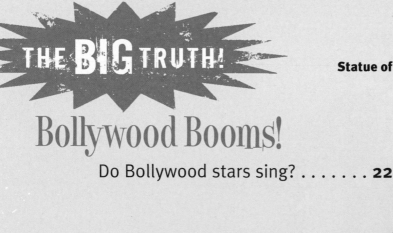

Statue of Buddha

The Palace of Winds in the city of Jaipur has 953 windows to let in the wind!

Mumbai apartment building

The Kumbh Mela is a huge religious festival that takes place in India every 12 years. In 2001, 17 million people took part. This broke the record for the world's biggest gathering.

CHAPTER 1

Land of Contrasts

As a country, India is hard to define. The country is relatively small, just about one-third the size of the United States. Yet in terms of its population, India is the second-largest country in the world. It has more than one billion people. India is the world's largest **democracy**.

India has so many people that it has set records for the world's largest gatherings.

India is a mixture of modern and ancient ways of life. It is a world leader in high-tech fields, but a great part of the population still leads very **traditional** lives. More than a million Indians are millionaires. Yet most people live on less than two dollars a day. India has more than 35 cities with populations of more than one million each. However, a majority of Indians live in **rural** communities.

Most Indians live in small farming villages. Markets are an important part of village life.

Tiger Survival

The Bengal tiger is India's national animal. These tigers were once found all over the country. Populations decreased as people hunted the tigers and destroyed their forest habitat. The tiger is now an endangered species. There are probably fewer than 4,000 wild tigers left in India. Hunters still sometimes kill them illegally for their skins. The Indian government has created a program called Project Tiger to try to save these big cats.

Temples at the Ki Gompa monastery have been built one on top of the other, for more than 1,000 years. The monastery is one of many in the Himalayas, the world's highest mountain range.

CHAPTER 2

Vast and Varied

India has great rivers and rocky deserts, vast plains and snow-capped mountains. Most of the land lies on a **peninsula** bordered by oceans. The Himalayan mountains rise in the northeast. In the northwest lies desert. The center of the country is a huge **plateau**. Plains run along the southern coasts.

The Himalayas are slowly growing taller, by almost an inch (2.5 centimeters) a year.

11

After monsoon rains, it is common for cities, such as Allahabad, to be flooded.

Climate

The climates of India range from the blazing heat of the deserts to the cool of the mountains. Weather is often extreme. Most of the country experiences monsoon winds in the late summer. These are seasonal winds that blow over the northern part of the Indian Ocean. They bring heavy rainfall.

Feeding Families

More than half the population survives by farming India's land. The country has long produced crops for **export,** such as tea, cashew nuts, and spices. Since the 1960s, the government has helped farmers grow more food for Indians. India is the world's largest producer of dried beans, such as kidney beans and chickpeas. It is one of the world's largest producers of rice and vegetables.

Tea grows well in India's hilly regions.

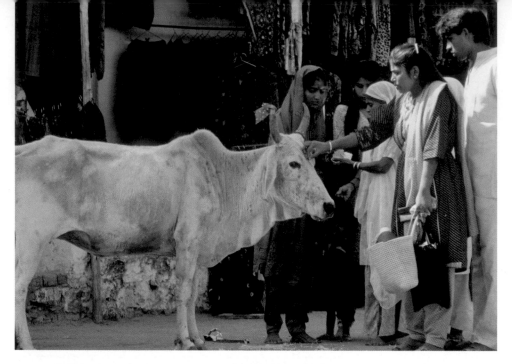

Cows freely roam the streets of India's cities. A cow's head is marked with a *tilak*, a Hindu symbol of good fortune.

Many Religions

For many Indians, religion is a big part of daily life. Most Indians are **Hindus.** Hinduism has many different gods. Hindus worship these gods at temples. They also have special altars in their homes for prayer. In Hinduism, cows are **sacred.** Many Hindus are vegetarians, which means they do not eat meat.

India has more than 150 million **Muslims**, or followers of Islam. Islam was founded in 622 c.e. in the area that is now Saudi Arabia. The religion has a long history in India. Muslim emperors ruled northern India for many years. Today, India has the second-largest Muslim population in the world, after Indonesia.

Mosques are Muslim places of worship. The Jama Masjid in Delhi is one of India's largest and most famous. Thousands of Muslims gather here to celebrate the end of Ramadan, a special month in the Muslim calendar.

Ancient Faiths

Besides Hindus and Muslims, India also has many people of other faiths. About 30 million Indians are Christians. Many others are **Buddhists**. The Buddhist religion began in India more than 2,500 years ago.

Sikhism began 500 years ago in India and is now the fifth-largest religion in the world. Sikhs follow the teachings of ten Gurus, or spiritual guides, who lived in north India between the 1400s and the 1700s.

The red robes these boys wear show that they are being educated at a Buddhist monastery. Often the oldest son of a Buddhist family will become a monk.

The Golden Temple of Amritsar is a holy place for Sikhs.

Two other common religions are Jainism and Zoroastrianism. India's four million Jains follow the teachings of ancient Jinas, or saints. Because they believe that all life is sacred, Jains are very strict vegetarians. Zoroastrians are followers of a religion that began thousands of years ago in Persia, in the Middle East.

This famous Hindu fortress is in the town of Gwalior in northern India. In 1858, a woman led Indian freedom fighters in a battle here against the British.

CHAPTER 3

Daily Life in India

Most Indian households are made up of extended families. Parents, children, and grandparents, and even uncles, aunts, and cousins, share a home. Often, a woman goes to live with her husband's household when she gets married. Child care and cooking responsibilities are usually shared by female members of the household.

Picnicking at historic sites is a popular outing for families in India.

Food and Fashion

Curry, a spicy stew, is a world famous dish of India. What people eat depends on where they live and their beliefs. People from northern India eat more meat than people in southern India. Most Indians use beans, rice, and many spices in their cooking.

Common Indian Spices

1. Bay leaf
2. Cardamom pods
3. Cardamom seeds
4. Cinnamon stick
5. Chili powder
6. Cloves
7. Cumin seeds
8. Curry powder
9. Garam masala
10. Peppercorns
11. Red chilies
12. Turmeric powder

Indian fashions are famous too, particularly the *saris* worn by many women. Traditional clothing for men includes the *dhoti* and the *lungi*. The *dhoti* is a piece of cloth tied up to form pants. The *lungi* is wrapped around the waist. Both men and women wear a long shirt called a *kurta*. This can be paired with pants in an outfit called a *salwar kameez*.

A sari is a single piece of fabric, worn wrapped around the body.

Bollywood Booms!

India has the world's largest movie industry, based in the city of Mumbai. The B in Bollywood comes from Bombay, the former name for Mumbai. Bollywood now makes more than 800 movies a year. That is about 300 more than Hollywood. An audience of around three billion people from around the world enjoys Bollywood movies.

Magical Music

Almost all Bollywood movies are musicals, with plenty of dancing. Their plots mix romance with comedy and drama. Many songs from Bollywood movies become superhits.

Singer or Actor?

Most Indian movie stars do not do their own singing. Instead, it's done by professionals called playback singers. Some playback singers even become stars in their own right.

These clay tablets may have printed some of the world's earliest labels. Indus Valley merchants probably used them to label their goods.

CHAPTER 4

The Path from the Past

Archaeologists still can't figure out how to read ancient Indus Valley writing.

Human beings have lived in India for tens of thousands of years. One of the world's oldest civilizations is the Indus Valley Civilization. It began more than 5,000 years ago, in what is now the country of Pakistan. Its high point was around 2,500 B.C.E. when it had many cities built out of brick and stone. **Archaeologists** are still learning about the Indus Valley, or Harappan, Civilization today.

After the decline of the Indus Valley Civilization, India had many different kingdoms and rulers. There were times of peace and prosperity with strong emperors, and periods of war and chaos. Temples were built, and Hindu art and culture flourished.

Around 1200 C.E., a Muslim general conquered northern India. Muslims would rule northern India for the next 500 years. A Muslim Empire known as the Mughal (MOH-guhl) Empire began in the 1500s. This great empire is known for its art and architecture.

Shah Jahan was a Mughal emperor. He is best remembered for building the Taj Mahal. This name means "crown of palaces."

Labor of Love

The Taj Mahal is India's most famous building. A Mughal emperor, filled with grief after the death of his wife, built the Taj Mahal as a monument to her. It was begun in the 1600s. It took 22 years and 20,000 workers to finish. Today it is considered a masterpiece of Muslim architecture. In 2007, the Taj Mahal was named one of the New Seven Wonders of the World.

Europeans in India

By 1600, India had been trading with Europe for more than 2,000 years. Spices and other goods from India were very valuable in Europe. Some European countries seized control of the valuable goods by invading India. In the 1500s, the Portuguese conquered parts of India. They established small colonies there. These colonies made the Portuguese very rich.

Time Line to Democracy

3000 B.C.E.
Some of the world's earliest great cities develop in the Indus Valley.

1500s
The Muslim Mughals rule northern India. They build the Red Fort at Agra and other great buildings.

Soon other European countries wanted part of that valuable trade. One of these countries was Great Britain. A company known as the British East India Company began setting up trading posts in India. The British had arrived. They would not leave India for another 350 years.

1858
Great Britain begins to govern India. Queen Victoria is named empress of India in 1876.

1947
India gains its independence. Today it is the world's largest democracy and a global leader in the high-tech industry.

Divide and Rule

At first, the British set up trade agreements with local Indian rulers. They would give the rulers money in exchange for the right to trade in their kingdoms. However, many Indian rulers borrowed money from the British and got into debt. The British also took advantage of wars between Indian rulers by siding with those who would give them the most power.

In 1901, King Edward of Britain became emperor of India. In 1903, a grand parade was held in Delhi in celebration.

This train station in Mumbai used to be named after Queen Victoria. She was the queen of England when it was built.

Many buildings in India were built in the British style.

Gradually, the British began taking over India, instead of just doing business there. The British Raj, the Indian word for "rule," lasted from 1858 to 1947. The British built railways and set up schools. They created a vast network of government employees to rule India. The legacy of the British Raj lives on in India today.

Mahatma Gandhi led a peaceful
struggle to free India from British rule.
His two grandnieces, shown here,
assisted him in his work.

CHAPTER 5

India Reborn

The history of India began to change dramatically in the early 1900s. This was largely due to one man, Mohandas K. Gandhi. Gandhi was a lawyer who lived in South Africa for many years. While there, he worked hard to end **discrimination** against Indians. Then, in 1915, he returned to India to help his own people gain independence from Great Britain.

Gandhi became known as Mahatma, which means "Great Soul" in the ancient Indian language, Sanskrit.

Most Indians were not happy with British rule. They wanted to govern themselves. Over the years, Indians tried many ways of overthrowing the British. Soldiers rose up against their commanders. Indian civilians refused to buy British goods. Nothing worked. India was very valuable to Great Britain, so the British were determined to stay.

Gandhi hated violence. He wanted to achieve independence peacefully. His campaigns were based on **civil disobedience**. He and his followers refused to obey unfair laws imposed by the British. They protested against these laws, and many were imprisoned for their acts of civil disobedience. For many years, Gandhi led thousands of Indians in acts of protest. His methods drew attention to British injustices. The British began to negotiate with Gandhi. In 1947, India gained independence from Great Britain.

A statue in New Delhi shows the famous salt march. In 1930, Gandhi led a 200-mile (322 km) march in protest against Great Britain's tax on salt. The British imprisoned more than 60,000 of the marchers.

Birth of Two Nations

The road to independence wasn't easy. Gandhi wanted all Indians to be part of the same country. However, Muslims and Hindus argued about the future of India. The Muslims persuaded the British to give them their own country. In 1947, two nations, India and Pakistan, were born.

At first, Pakistan had two parts, East and West Pakistan. In 1971, East Pakistan became the independent nation of Bangladesh. West Pakistan is now simply called Pakistan.

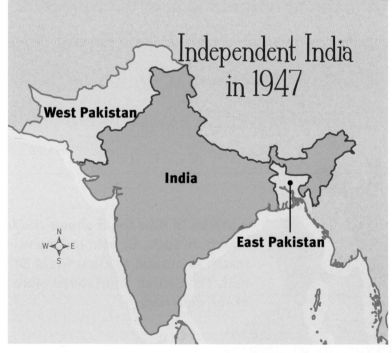

Independent India in 1947

West Pakistan

India

East Pakistan

N
W E
S

Many Muslims living in India moved to Pakistan. Many Hindus from Pakistan moved to India. During this time, violence broke out in both countries. Hundreds of thousands were killed. Gandhi worked with many religious leaders to calm the anger. However, in 1948 Gandhi was shot and killed.

A Violent Attack

In November 2008, a group of armed men attacked sites across the the city of Mumbai. After three days of explosions and gunfire, at least 195 people were killed and hundreds more were injured. Some officials believe the attackers were terrorists from Pakistan. Terrorists use violence to frighten others, often for political reasons. India has now further strenghtened its security throughout the nation.

This Baha'i temple in New Delhi was opened in 1986. The Baha'i faith began in 1844 in Iraq. This temple welcomes people of all religions.

CHAPTER 6

India Today

The Lotus Temple is shaped like a lotus flower. Its 27 "petals" are covered in marble.

Today, India remains a true mix of the traditional and the modern. Many Indians still live in homes made of mud. They collect water from a well. They grow their crops the same way their ancestors did. Life is much the same as it was 100 years ago, except for one thing—technology. These days, cars and mopeds share roads with buffalo carts. At night, huts are lit up from the glow of televisions.

Cybercafes can be found in most big cities in India, such as New Delhi. There are more than 200,000 Internet cafes across India.

Other Indians live in an increasingly high-tech world. The city of Hyderabad (hy-duhr-uh-BAD) has earned the nickname Cyberabad. This is because it has so many cybercafes and high-tech companies. City dwellers can choose from more than 500 Indian cable TV channels. They go to work in gleaming new office buildings. They talk to each other on cell phones.

Many Indians are very modern in the way they eat, live, and dress. However, social and religious traditions continue to shape people's lives. Many marriages are arranged by the parents of the bride and groom. Some Indian newlyweds choose to live with the husband's family.

Marigold flowers are used as decorations for Hindu marriages. They are a symbol of good fortune and happiness.

A World Power

Educated Indians have many career opportunities. The international high-tech industry provides work in banks, call centers, IT companies, or animation studios. Medicine, science, and engineering are also growing fields.

What will India be like 50 years from now? That's a hard question to answer. India is rapidly changing. It is becoming increasingly modern. It is gaining more international power. Who knows where the world's largest democracy will go from here? ★

Education has improved in today's India. The number of Indians who can read and write has gone up by 40 percent since 1960.

True Statistics

Official name: Republic of India

Size: About 1,270,000 sq. mi. (3,290,000 sq. km)

Major Cities: New Delhi (the capital), Mumbai, Kolkata, Chennai, Bengaluru, Hyderabad, Ahmedabad, Pune

Official languages: 15

Population: About 1,148,000,000

Highest point: Kangchenjunga Mountain, about 28,208 ft. (8,598 m)

Currency: Indian rupee

Internet country code: IN

Thali platter

Did you find the truth?

T Many Indians don't eat meat.

F The elephant is India's national animal.

Resources

Books

Brownlie Bojang, Ali, and Nicola Barber. *Focus on India*. Milwaukee, WI: World Almanac Library, 2007.

Chatterjee, Manini, and Anita Roy. *India (Eyewitness Books)*. New York: Dorling Kindersley, 2002.

Dalal, A. Kamala. *India* (Countries of the World). Washington, DC: National Geographic, 2007.

Heydlauff, Lisa, and Nitin Upadhye. *Going to School in India*. Watertown, MA: Charlesbridge, 2005.

Johnson, Robin, and Bobbie Kalman. *Spotlight on India* (Spotlight on My Country). New York: Crabtree Publishing, 2008.

Schomp, Virginia. *Ancient India* (People of the Ancient World). New York: Franklin Watts, 2005.

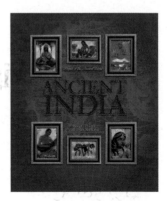

Organizations and Web Sites

India and its Neighbors
www.sscnet.ucla.edu/southasia/
Learn about all aspects of India, from geography to culture.

The Indus Civilization
www.harappa.com/har/haro.html
Explore one of the world's most ancient civilizations.

Kids for Tigers
www.sanctuaryasia.com/kidsfortigers/
Read about children in India who are finding creative ways
to help save the rare Bengal tiger.

Places to Visit

Asian Art Museum
200 Larkin Street
San Francisco, CA 94102
(415) 581 3500
www.asianart.org/
See the different faiths of
India expressed in 2,000
years of art.

Museum of Fine Arts, Boston
465 Huntington Avenue
Boston, MA 02115-5597
(617) 267 9300
www.mfa.org/
Marvel at magnificent Mughal
miniatures in a big collection
of Indian paintings.

Important Words

archaeologist (ar-kee-OL-uh-jist) – a scientist who learns about people of the past by studying ancient objects

Buddhist – a person who follows the teachings of Buddha

civil disobedience – choosing not to obey laws, as a form of political protest

democracy (di-MOK-ruh-see) – a form of government in which the people choose their leaders in elections

discrimination – unfair treatment based on differences such as age, race, class, or gender

export – the act of sending goods to another country to be sold there

Hindu – a person who follows Hinduism, an ancient religious and cultural tradition that has a belief in many gods

Muslim – a person who believes in a single god and follows the teachings of the Prophet Muhammad

peninsula – land that juts into the sea from the mainland

plateau (pla-TOH) – an area of raised, flat land

rural – relating to the countryside and the people who live there

sacred – having to do with religion; important or deserving respect

traditional (truh-DISH-uh-nuhl) – relating to customs or beliefs handed down from one generation to the next

Index

Page numbers in **bold** indicate illustrations

About the Author

Sunita Apte always knew she wanted to be a writer. She grew up in North Carolina with an Indian father and a Hungarian mother. She also lived for a year in Chennai (formerly Madras) as a child. That year abroad sparked a lifelong love of travel. When she is not writing children's books at home in Brooklyn, Sunita travels the world with her family. India is one of her favorite places to visit, since she has many aunts and cousins to see there.